LEARN TO PLAY THE
DRUMS

LEARN TO PLAY THE
DRUMS

Simon Bridgestock

PaRragon

Bath · New York · Singapore · Hong Kong · Cologne · Delhi · Melbourne

First published by Parragon in 2009
Parragon
Queen Street House
4 Queen Street
Bath BA1 1HE, UK

Designed, produced, and packaged by
Stonecastle Graphics Ltd

Text by Simon Bridgestock
Designed by Sue Pressley and Paul Turner
Edited by Philip de Ste. Croix
Editorial consultant Nick Freeth
Drum notation diagrams by Nick Freeth
Picture research by Karen James

ISBN 978-1-4075-5566-9

Printed in Malaysia

Contents

Introduction   6

Chapter 1

The Drum Set   **8**

Origins of the Drum Set   10

Notable Players   12

Anatomy of the Drum Set   14

Tools of the Trade   16

Tuning Your Drums   18

Chapter 2

Getting Started   **20**

Notes and Rests   22

Understanding the Musical Stave   24

Dynamics   26

Quarters, Eighths, and Sixteenths   28

About Triplets   30

Grip and Posture   32

Strokes   34

Chapter 3

Rudiments   **36**

The Building Blocks for Your Chops   38

Single Stroke Rolls   40

Double Stroke Rolls and Variations   42

The Diddle   44

Flams   46

Drags   48

Multiple Bounce Roll   50

Chapter 4

Your First Beat   **52**

The Eighth Note Beat—1   54

The Eighth Note Beat—2   56

The Eighth Note Beat—3   58

Chapter 5

Adding To The Beat   **60**

Counting Sixteenths—1   62

Counting Sixteenths—2   64

Counting Sixteenths—3   66

Chapter 6

Moving On   **68**

Triplets and Shuffles   70

Fills   72

Other Styles   74

Final Pieces   76

Epilogue   78

Index   80

Introduction

The drums, in some form or another, are perhaps the oldest of all musical instruments. From the drums of ancient Africa to today's sophisticated drum sets, they appeal to people from all cultures and musical traditions. Without the rhythms that these instruments produce, music would be very different to the aural experience we know and love today.

The drums are capable of an incredible array of sounds and textures. Just compare the character of modern rock drums to the complex polyrhythms of the Indian tabla, or the sophistication of jazz drumming and the electronic sounds of drum 'n' bass to appreciate this amazing diversity.

This book is mainly concerned with what is known as the modern drum set and the styles of drumming associated with it. It will introduce you to the basics of the instrument and with a little application you will soon be drumming to your favorite songs with confidence. From there on it's up to you—if you can apply yourself, you will never stop learning.

It will cover all the important aspects to get you started straight away, but don't worry if you don't initially have a drum kit at your disposal because you can still learn from the exercises—all you need are a pair of sticks and something to hit!

The first section of the book gives an overview of the drum set, its history and greatest players, information on what type of kit to buy, its constituent parts and useful accessories. It then describes the essential basic techniques concerning posture and the various grips and strokes you will need to master.

Learning music notation can seem a daunting prospect, and, yes, even drummers read music! However, Chapter 2 is designed to remove the stress from this process, and you will be reading notation confidently in no time.

Before looking at the beats themselves, there is a chapter covering the rudiments, which form the basis of every good drummer's practice. These are incredibly important for developing the skills required to become a drummer, whatever the style of music you choose.

Then on to the good stuff—the grooves themselves! Each exercise is designed to develop your drumming vocabulary and technique. At the end of the book you will find some more varied and unusual beats to try out.

It is recommended that you work through each part of the book in sequence to obtain the best results. Everyone learns at a different pace, but with enthusiasm, patience, and lots of practice you will achieve a great deal surprisingly quickly.

Above: The Indian tradition of tabla playing dates back to the 18th century and is an integral part of Indian classical music.

Opposite above: This is a fully specified modern drum set, played here by Stewart Copeland of The Police. Note the plethora of equipment.

Opposite: Traditional African drumming. The modern drum set we know today has evolved from drums like these.

No drum book can claim to cover every aspect of the subject, and this book is no exception. The intention is that you should use it as a springboard for further study, either in book form or by seeking tuition from an experienced tutor. However, this short introduction to a huge subject will give you, the beginner, a great start to your drumming career.

Deciding to learn an instrument is no small undertaking, but neither should it be totally stressful. Learning to drum should be fun, and with that sense of pleasure comes the enthusiasm to apply yourself to discovering and mastering this great instrument.

It's time to turn the page and begin your journey into the world of drumming...

Chapter 1

The Drum Set

The beginner to drumming has many things to consider. What type of set should I go for? Which sticks do I need? What cymbals do I buy? When starting out you will have a million questions on your mind. This section explains exactly what you need to get started. But first, let's begin with a little history…

Origins of the Drum Set

Although rhythmic instruments have been around for thousands of years, the modern drum kit or "set" has developed only relatively recently. The story of modern drums really began in the late 19th century in New Orleans, a city rich with a varied population of migrating peoples, many of whom came from Europe and Africa.

One of the dominant musical traditions at this time was military music and it was often embodied by the marching band. Here the melodic styles of Europe combined with the rhythmic pulse of African drumming.

Initially, the drummers comprised snare players and bass drum players. The instruments were played upright as the band marched through the streets of New Orleans. Soon, these bands began to play indoors in the famous clubs and theaters of the city's red light district, Storyville, where they performed early types of jazz music.

There was no need to march once the band had moved indoors (there certainly wasn't the space), so through necessity a player had to play both the snare and bass drum simultaneously. This style became known as "double drumming." Drummers then began to add all sorts of weird and wonderful extras—cymbals, temple blocks, and early forms of tom-toms. These early setups were called "traps" (from "contraption").

As the popularity of these bands increased, new technical developments quickly followed. The bass drum pedal was invented in 1895 by Dee Dee Chandler and then refined by William F. Ludwig around 1909. This pedal enabled the drum (now placed on its side) to be struck via a pedal controlled by the player's foot and so freed up his hands to introduce other sounds.

In 1926 the hi-hat pedal appeared. This enabled two raised cymbals to be opened and closed by the player's foot and create short, staccato-like

sounds when the cymbals closed. The player could also use sticks to play rhythmic patterns on them.

Cymbals were originally of Asiatic origin and there is evidence of their use as far back as 1100 BC. Some designs were flat, but the most common design incorporates a "dome" at the center point, nowadays referred to as the bell. Today a drum set will consist of a "ride" cymbal for marking out time (especially in jazz forms) and a "crash" normally used for punctuating the beat to add drama to the music. Other cymbals include a "splash," which is smaller than the crash, and the "China," which has a trashier sound.

Tom-tom drums are believed to have developed from Chinese Pieng ku drums and/or Native American drums, although no one is sure of their exact provenance. They are perhaps the oldest

Above: Throughout the ages drums have been used in rituals and festivals and as vital means of communication in times of war, as can be seen in this detailed 16th-century French painting.

DRUM FACT
The technical term for a drum (a cylinder with a stretched "skin" across the top and bottom, which produces sound by vibrating) is "membranophone."

DRUM HISTORY

The earliest known percussion instrument dates back to around 15,000 years ago. Found in the Ukraine, it is made from a hollow mammoth skull and it would presumably have had an animal skin stretched tightly over the top.

By the 1960s as the popularity of jazz music waned and rock 'n' roll took center stage, the young, new drummers often carried on with this setup but also continued to innovate. Ringo Starr from The Beatles and Keith Moon from The Who both played this classic kit design. Cream's Ginger Baker added a second bass drum and extra toms. By the 1980s drums had diversified into many configurations. The double bass drum pedal became popular (for thrash metal in particular) and drummers, such as Bill Bruford and Pat Mastelloto, added electronic drum pads to their acoustic kits to extend their sonic palettes. Today there is an almost inexhaustible range of options for the drummer; some continue to innovate with large and complex setups while others have returned to the classic designs of old.

The drum set is a truly international instrument, having derived its constituent parts from virtually every corner of the globe. Today, its many forms continue to develop as the musical climate evolves—it has come a long way from its humble origins as a customized mammoth skull!

Left: A street festival in Naha, Okinawa, Japan, where ancient traditions are still revered and practiced. Here the "Sanshin" drums are played by up to 30 players.

Below: Toby Foyeh and Orchestra Africa from Nigeria fuse modern and traditional percussion instruments. Here their conga player lays down a groove.

form of drum that would have been used not only musically, but also as a form of communication, perhaps to herald the advance of an enemy or to celebrate his defeat. Today they survive as an integral part of the modern drum set.

The drumheads (or skins on the drums) have evolved from older animal-skin-based types (such as calfskin) to today's advanced synthetic types produced from polyester or Kevlar. Some have a smooth, clear surface while others are coated with a rougher surface, which are particularly useful for brushwork.

In the 1930s, the great jazz drummer Gene Krupa became known for his basic four-piece kit, which became the standard configuration for many years to come. It consisted of a bass drum, snare, one bass-drum-mounted tom-tom, and a free-standing floor tom, hi-hat, and rim-mounted cymbals.

Notable Players

Technical innovations to the drum set have developed side by side with the musical innovations of the players themselves. In every generation there have been stand-out players of incredible talent who inspire the next generation that follows them. Here we will take a brief look at some great players of the past and present.

and individual style, though not flash or showy, perfectly complements the songs of Lennon and McCartney or George Harrison.

Keith Moon

Moon's eccentric behavior is well known, but The Who's drummer was also a great exponent of the instrument whose loud playing still serves as a template for rock drummers everywhere.

John Bonham

Perhaps the greatest of the classic rock drummers. Bonham, who played with Led Zeppelin, infused his heavy (and very loud) grooves with a large slice of funk. His beats are still being sampled today. Highlights include the intro to "When The Levee Breaks" and "Kashmir."

Left: The master jazz drummer Buddy Rich shown here playing his trademark Slingerland drum set. He inspired many of the next generation.

Buddy Rich

Buddy Rich was a child prodigy on the drums and was known as "Traps the drum wonder." He matured into a virtuoso big band jazz drummer and leader, where his explosive style won great respect. In 1966 he recorded the *West Side Story* medley, which has since become one of his best-known works.

Clyde Stubblefield

Ex-James Brown drummer Stubblefield is one of the most sampled drummers of all time. His seminal funk grooves can be heard on "Cold Sweat" and "Funky Drummer."

Ringo Starr

Ringo Starr is probably one of the world's most famous rock drummers, having been an integral part of the fab four, The Beatles. His inventive

Left: The great showman Keith Moon here demonstrates his drumming skills and his penchant for theatrics.

SNARE ORIGINS
The snare can trace its origins back to the medieval "tabor," which is still used in certain forms of European folk music.

Airto Moreira

Brazilian-born Moreira showed an amazing aptitude for drums from an early age. At thirteen he became a professional musician. A master of Latin percussion, he has played with many of the great Latin and jazz performers, including Chick Corea, Joe Zawinul, Hermeto Pascoal, and many more. The album *Return To Forever* by Chick Corea's band of the same name demonstrates his brilliance at Latin drum set playing.

Billy Cobham

Famous for his incredible powerhouse technique that was at once frenetic but very accurate, Cobham originally came to prominence playing with jazz trumpeter giant Miles Davis and then found fame with the fusion group Mahavishnu Orchestra in the 1970s (fusion meaning the combining of jazz, rock, and other styles). His solo album *Spectrum* is a master class in fusion drumming. Incidentally, he is the drummer on the theme from *Hawaii Five-0*!

Terry Bozzio

Famed for his work with Frank Zappa, Bozzio is regarded as one of the great technicians. He pioneered the "melodic ostinato" style, where he plays a repeating figure with his feet, then solos with his hands (and sometimes in reverse). His drum clinic performances are always sold out. Check out his *Solo Drum Music I-III* and Zappa's *Joe's Garage*.

Stewart Copeland

The Police drummer has a very distinctive style that mixes rock forms along with reggae-style grooves. "Driven To Tears" on the Police album *Zenyatta Mondatta* is a good example of his tight, syncopated playing.

Dave Grohl

Although now known for his work with Foo Fighters as lead singer and guitarist, Grohl was Nirvana's drummer. His modern "grunge" rock style has influenced many players of today.

Keith Carlock

A highly respected session drummer from New York, Carlock has played with Steely Dan, Diana Ross, and Sting. He is considered an all-round drummer, capable of playing in many styles, which is a prerequisite for any session musician. Listen to Steely Dan's *Everything Must Go* album to hear his stylish, modern groove playing.

SNARE DRUM FACT
The snare drum is so called because a strip of wavy metal wire (the snare itself) is stretched tightly across the bottom skin, or resonant head. When the drum is hit, this snare vibrates against the resonant skin to give the drum its characteristic "fizzy" sound.

Anatomy of the Drum Set

The drum kit is really a collection of smaller instruments that function in unison. Here the conventional names for each of these components are explained. Memorizing these names will familiarize you with the elements of a drum kit and help when you get to figuring out drum notation.

Drums come in all shapes and sizes. Bass drums, for example, are available in various dimensions and they have different applications, depending on the needs and tastes of the player.

As with the bass drum, there are many choices of snare available to the player. Some are made from brass, some of quality woods, such as maple or birch. Some are deeper than others to produce a louder sound, while the piccolo snare with its shallow shell is popular in drum 'n' bass music.

The variety of choice can be bewildering for a newbie, but a good place to start would be to acquire a set similar to the one shown here. The beauty of drum sets is that you can add to them as your needs and predilections develop.

Although it is preferable to buy new, it is possible to obtain good bargains secondhand, although you must be wary of any faults. Make sure all the tension rods are present and that the snare springs (under the snare drum) aren't broken. Broken

Ride Cymbal **Crash Cymbal** **Tom-Tom** **Hi-Hat** **Snare** **Floor Tom** **Bass Drum**

TYPES OF DRUM SET

Jazz Kit
This is the classic setup. It usually has one mounted tom on the bass drum and two floor toms.

Rock Kit
With two mounted toms and one floor tom, the rock kit is the most commonly seen style of kit.

Heavy Metal Kit
With a proliferation of toms, the heavy metal kit is sometimes beefed up with two bass drums and as many cymbals as possible!

Electronic Kit
These kits derive their sounds from a "brain," that is a sound module which uses synthesized or sampled sounds which are triggered by hitting the pads.

drumheads or skins are acceptable because they can be easily replaced (in fact it is always a good idea to re-skin your drums if they are bought secondhand). Cosmetic imperfections, such as shell scratches, will not affect the sound, but look out for any cracks and rust. You never know, you may discover a vintage classic that has been lying hidden in someone's basement!

Your local music store should stock a selection of kits, although the Internet can offer some great bargains. However, it is preferable to see your kit before you buy and your local supplier should be able to give you some sound advice. Many beginner kits will also provide a set of cymbals, although be aware that with some more expensive sets you will only get the drums—the cymbals must be purchased separately.

Above: If you have space restrictions and/or concerns about volume, then an electronic set is a great alternative. Unlike real drums you can use headphones to listen to the sound.

Right: An overhead view of a standard drum set with each part named. The most common configuration is two mounted toms and one floor tom, but each player will build his or her drum set according to personal preference.

Opposite: A side-on view of a jazz drum set with its constituent parts named. A jazz set usually has one mounted tom and one or two floor toms.

Crash Cymbal

Tom-Tom

Bass Drum

Ride Cymbal

Hi-Hat

Floor Toms

Hi-Hat Pedal

Snare

Bass Drum Pedal

Splash Cymbal

Drum Throne

Tools of the Trade

Once you've got your shiny (or not so shiny) drum set, there are a multitude of options for you to consider, and each "tool" will enable you to achieve many different sounds with your set. There are also a number of accessories that you may want to acquire. If used as part of your regular practice, they will become integral to your development.

Sticks

Drumsticks come in all shapes and sizes and there are no hard and fast rules as to what will suit you. Generally speaking the fatter they are, the more suited they are to heavier, louder forms of music, such as metal and thrash. Lighter sticks might lend themselves to lighter forms, such as jazz or Latin styles. It is up to you to decide which size stick to use, although for practice purposes a heavier stick can help to improve your technique.

Your local music store should have a broad selection of sticks available, so spend some time when choosing. What may suit you initially may change over time. The most important point to be aware of is that the sticks are well balanced in terms of weight and not warped. A good way to test this is to roll the sticks on a flat surface to see if there are any imperfections.

There are many stick sizes to choose from and they are usually coded with a number followed by a letter, for example, "7A" or "5B." There are three letter codings: "S" (largest size), "B" (medium size), and "A" (smallest size). The smaller the number, the greater the width within the letter coding.

Multirods

Multirods fall somewhere between sticks and brushes. They are made up of thin rods bound together. Generally made from plastic or wood, they offer a softer alternative to sticks and more attack than brushes.

Brushes

Brushes are most commonly used in jazz, but they shouldn't be written off as only appropriate to that genre of music because they offer a different, subtle texture not achievable with sticks.

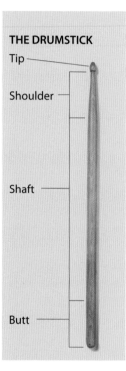

THE DRUMSTICK

- Tip
- Shoulder
- Shaft
- Butt

Far left: Wooden drumsticks are usually made of oak, hickory, or hard maple.

Left: Multirods are often made of birch dowel.

Left and right: Brushes create a soft style which is good for jazz and ballad playing.

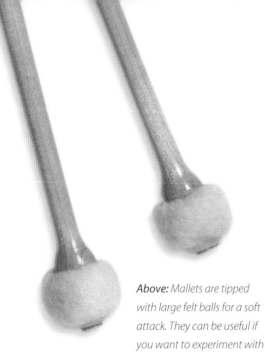

Above: Mallets are tipped with large felt balls for a soft attack. They can be useful if you want to experiment with different sounds.

Mallets

Classical percussionists who play on timpani and other percussion instruments often use these sticks with larger, softer heads. They are used by jazz and rock drummers to create softer, more atmospheric textures. For example, mallets are particularly useful for creating cymbal "swells."

Useful Accessories

Once you've chosen your kit and sticks, you might want to consider investing in some extra items that will assist you in practice and performance.

Protect Your Ears

One of the main drawbacks with the drums is the incredible volume of sound that they can produce when played at full tilt. It's not just your neighbors you have to consider, but your own hearing too. Prolonged exposure to high sound volumes will damage your ears over time and, as a musician, that's the last thing you want to happen. One way round this, apart from playing more quietly (although that is recommended), is to buy some earplugs. Basic earplugs are inexpensive and they will filter out the dangerous sound frequencies that can lead to hearing loss. The disadvantage of them is that they can make your perception of the kit "muffled." More sophisticated earplugs are available that give you a more realistic sound, but they are more expensive.

Get in Time

Apart from being noisy, the drummer's most important job is to play "in time." No one wants a drummer who slows down or speeds up when the song doesn't require it. An essential piece of your kit that will improve your time-keeping capabilities is the metronome. Highly recommended is an electronic type to which you can attach earphones. Because of the loud volume that the drums produce, you will have no trouble in hearing them over the click of the metronome. Many electronic sets also include a built-in metronome.

Pads

If, like many of us, you have neighbors or family members who are going to tire of a drum kit being played at all hours, then you might want to get yourself a practice pad or set. These rubber pads maintain the bounce of real drums but are virtually silent. They are highly recommended for practicing your basic skills without annoying everyone around you.

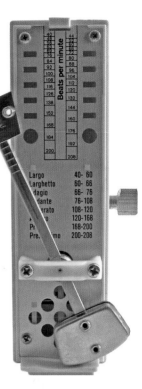

Above: A traditional metronome, which is essential to all drummers for good practice of the basics. Electronic versions are also available.

Left and above: Earplugs will protect your ears while drumming, and a practice pad will enable you to occasionally practice in virtual silence.

Tuning Your Drums

Before you begin to play, it is worth taking some time to tune your drum set.
Tuning is a matter of personal taste, and although there is no definitively right or wrong
way to go about this, there are some basic rules to observe that will point you in the
right direction.

Each drum has its own pitch, for example whether it sounds high or low in the scale. Conventionally the smallest tom is the highest and the remaining drums range down to the bass drum, with its low thud. When tuning your drum it's a good idea to follow this process:

Detune the drumhead or skin by loosening the tension rods with the drum key. You can now completely remove and discard the old head. It is also a good idea at this point to clean around the rim to remove any dust.

Now place the new head on the drum cylinder and replace the tension rods and turn them by half a turn.

Press down on the head with the palm of your hands to loosen up the head.

Detune the head again.

Then, using the diagram opposite, tune each tension rod by a quarter turn until the desired pitch is achieved. Tap the head near the rods to compare the pitch across the drum—if they are all the same pitch and you like the sound, then you are ready to go!

Tuning your drums is a matter of trial and error and it might take a few attempts until you are happy with the sound. Remember—if it sounds good, then it is good!

Left: Detune the head by loosening the tension rods.

Left: Place the new head on the drum cylinder and replace the tension rods.

Left: Press down on the head with the palm of your hand.

Tuning the Tension Rods

Above: In this diagram the snare's tuning rods have been numbered. Begin with number 1, then move opposite to rod 2 and so on until all the rods have been tightened. Tap the drum as you go and repeat until you are happy with the overall sound.

Above: A standard rock drum set with two mounted toms and a single floor tom. Start by tuning the first tom, then the second, followed by the floor tom. Aim for clearly defined pitch differences.

Right: A classic heavy metal-style drum set. The principles of tuning remain the same, but make sure the bass drums are tuned to the same pitch.

TUNING AN ELECTRONIC DRUM SET

An electronic drum set comes packed with hundreds of sounds that are derived from "samples," which are real recordings of drum sounds that are loaded into the memory of the sound module, or "brain." These are usually of a very high quality and sound great straight out of the box. However, depending on the particular make of electronic drums, it is possible to edit, or "tune," the sounds to create your own unique set, and once you are happy with the sound's pitch, the results may be saved as user presets for a number of different players.

Chapter 2
Getting Started

*Understanding the concepts of written drum notation
is not as frightening as it might first seem to a beginner.
When seen as an aid that helps in the practical application
of your skills, it becomes an important element in your
learning. This chapter will gently guide you through the
early stages of reading notation. We will also take a look
at the basic techniques of drumming. You may not think it,
but simply learning how to hold the sticks and to achieve
correct posture is the crucial first stage in learning to drum.
Incorrect technique could hamper your development and
even cause you physical discomfort.*

Notes and Rests

Music notation—writing down the notes you have to play—is the most common and easiest way to communicate musical ideas. It is also a great way for the new drummer to understand how rhythm really works. Here we take a look at what the symbols used in drum notation mean.

This chapter contains information that you may not have come across before. Try not to feel intimidated by the terminology and take your time reading it carefully. You may not take everything in at once, so you can use this chapter as a reference to which you can return as needed. The exercises later on in the book will slowly introduce you to reading rhythm and you will discover that it is not as complicated as it might first seem. In fact, it is a logical and neat way to notate drum music.

Notes

Each individual name describes the length of the note, which is particularly useful when reading rhythm. The longest note 𝅝 is called a whole note (this is also known as a semibreve).

A count of "1,2,3,4" equals a whole note.

All the other notes are divisions of that whole note (see example, above right). It is perhaps helpful to imagine the whole note as a pie, with each successive note being a smaller portion of that pie. In the accompanying diagram the notes are represented as a "tree." You can clearly see here how all the notes emerge as subdivisions from the whole note, which sits at the top.

For example, the half note (or minim) is half a whole note (semibreve), so two half notes can fit into one whole note.

Quarter notes (or crotchets) are half as long again, so four quarter notes can fit into one whole note and so on.

Lengths of Notes: The Note Tree

Right: This diagram illustrates how the primary whole note is subdivided into smaller—or to be precise—shorter notes on the branches beneath. Each successive note is half the length of the preceding note.

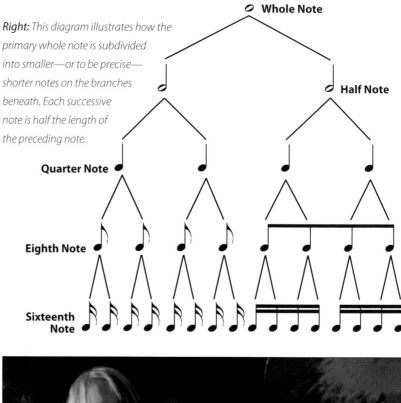

Rests are of equal importance to the notes in written music. They tell you when not to play—when a silence is required in the musical piece. They represent different note lengths in exactly the same way as the notes but they use different symbols.

Look at this table, right, and try to memorize the note and rest values.

Drum Notation Legend

In drum notation each part of the kit is described using specific symbols. Instead of the notes on the grid of lines representing pitch (as they do in conventional musical notation), they represent parts of your drum set. Below is a diagram showing the symbol for each part of the kit.

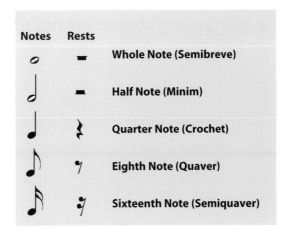

Notes	Rests	
𝅝	▬	**Whole Note (Semibreve)**
𝅗𝅥	▬	**Half Note (Minim)**
♩	𝄽	**Quarter Note (Crochet)**
♪	𝄾	**Eighth Note (Quaver)**
𝅘𝅥𝅯	𝄿	**Sixteenth Note (Semiquaver)**

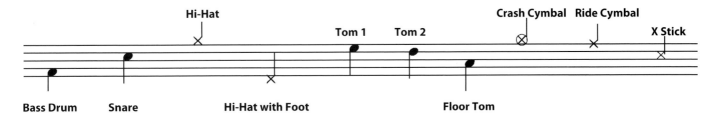

Hi-Hat Tom 1 Tom 2 Crash Cymbal Ride Cymbal X Stick

Bass Drum Snare Hi-Hat with Foot Floor Tom

BEAMING

Sometimes, when there are many notes grouped within the same beat, it is a good idea to tie them together for clarity. The use of beaming, in which horizontal lines, or "beams," join notes together, helps to make the musical piece more readable.

Opposite: Understanding the note lengths will greatly assist your progress on the drum set.

X STICK

Cross-stick, or X stick is an alternative way to play the snare. Place the stick across the head so that the tip rests in the center and the shaft rests on the rim of the drum. Play it only by lifting the part that's outside the drum. This method can be used in any style of music, but is prominent in reggae, Latin, and jazz.

Left: When learning to play the drums, there is a lot to take in at first, but it will be a lot of fun, so don't be too daunted by the unfamiliar terminology.

Understanding the Musical Stave

Like conventionally written music, drum notation uses a stave and notes. However, these do not represent pitch as such, but parts of the drum set, as explained on the previous pages. Here we look more closely at the stave and its constituent parts.

Measures and Bar Lines

Here we have the musical stave. The stave is made up of five horizontal lines upon which notes are placed. The spaces between the lines are also used.

The stave

Imagine the stave as a musical time line on which certain musical events will take place. It is usually divided using bar lines to represent "measures" within the time line. A measure or bar is a section that contains the beats—normally a set amount—that are to be played.

There are three types of bar line to remember:

Single Bar Line
The most commonly used bar line that divides up the measures into boxes.

Double Bar Line
These are used to signify the end of a particular section.

Fine Bar Line
Used at the end of the musical composition. Pronounced "fee nay."

Time Signatures

Time signatures are the two fractionlike figures that you see at the beginning of a stave. They tell you two things—how many beats or counts there are in a measure and the length of each beat.

The top number tells you how many beats there are to a bar, the bottom the length of each beat.

The 4/4 Time Signature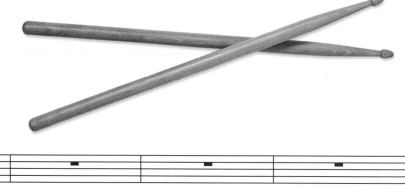

The above example shows 4/4, which, because of its popularity throughout music, is often referred to as "common time."

This time signature shows that there are four beats to the bar (the top number), and that each note is a quarter note (the bottom number).

Most popular Western music uses this time, and 3/4 is also very popular, in waltz music, for example. This means there are three beats to the bar—"1,2,3, 1,2,3"—and each beat is a quarter note long.

Above: A music stand is a useful accessory, enabling you to view the music notation with ease.

You will encounter other time signatures as you progress, such as 5/4 (a good example of this would be Dave Brubeck's "Take Five"), 7/4, 9/4, and others. In Arabic music odd time signatures are commonplace, but in the West we tend to keep things more simple!

The Clef

Other instruments, such as the piano or guitar, use a "clef" at the beginning of a piece to denote the register in which the piece is to be played. You may have come across the treble clef and bass clef before.

For drums the percussion clef is used and commonly looks like this:

The Percussion Clef

Repeats

Repeat brackets are often used to denote when a passage needs to be played again.

Repeats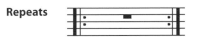

Below: Once you have understood the musical stave and become familiar with its symbols, you will find progress much easier.

Dynamics

If you have ever tapped a drum before, you may have noticed that the harder you hit the skin surface, the louder the note, but if struck softly you will hear a quieter note. This difference in volume, when used musically, is called dynamics. Dynamics in music notation describe the differences in volume between different notes.

Dynamics can create great subtlety and drama in any musical phrase or piece. Traditionally dynamics are described using Italian words that signify one of six volume levels (see Dynamic Markings table, right). These dynamic events are achieved depending on how hard you hit the drum or cymbal. This is accomplished by adjusting the stick height prior to the stroke. The higher the stick, the louder the sound you will make, and vice versa.

Gradual or sudden volume changes are described in these ways:

Crescendo
Here the musical phrase increases in volume.

Decrescendo
The opposite of crescendo, also known as diminuendo. The phrase gets softer.

Accents
Prescribed to individual notes, indicating a sudden volume increase.

Ghost Notes, or Grace Notes
The opposite of accents. Notes are de-emphasized, and sometimes are almost silent.

Without dynamics, music would be a very monotonous and uninspiring experience. The differences in volume can help to tell a musical story as much as the melody or words can. Using different dynamic levels is an integral part of understanding how music works for any musician, be they a singer, pianist, or drummer.

DYNAMIC MARKINGS		
ff	fortissimo	very loud
f	forte	loud
mf	mezzo-forte	moderately loud
mp	mezzo-piano	moderately soft
p	piano	soft
pp	pianissimo	very soft

A simple, yet very effective, example of this is Nirvana's "Smells Like Teen Spirit." In the song the verses are "pulled" back volume-wise. Sound levels begin to build in the pre-chorus, then, as the chorus arrives, the band plays at full tilt, which creates an exciting, powerful effect. Imagine this song if it was played at the same volume throughout, and I think you'll agree that it would lose much of its distinctive character.

Above: Here the hi-hat is struck a quarter way from the tip of the drumstick to make a thicker, louder sound.

The drummer in particular is capable of executing the extremes of the dynamic range, and many drummers will use this effectively throughout the duration of a song. A drum roll on the tom-toms before a chorus or at the end of the song, or the crash of a cymbal at the beginning of a bar are often played more loudly than the preceding and following beats. In this way, the drummer can add points of interest that can underpin the message or emotion of a song.

These dynamic changes can occur suddenly, or gradually. Listen to Ravel's *Bolero* to hear how a whole musical piece can develop over an extended period of time. This exhilarating composition begins very softly and increases in volume through a powerful crescendo. Note: This piece is also famous for its repetitive snare pattern that does not change throughout.

For every loud dynamic note there is a quieter counterpart. The opposite of an accent is a ghost, or grace note. Without this opposition there can be no dynamics. It is a simple, yet essential, part of music.

To create these differences in volume, the drummer can use different sticking heights. Start by lifting a stick to shoulder height and then let it drop onto, for example, a snare drum. This creates a loud note. Next, place your stick 2 inches (5cm) above the same drum and let it drop. This will create a much quieter note. It is also softer in its "attack." The louder note will not only be louder, but its sonic character will be sharper (this is problematic to describe in words, so try it for yourself to see what I mean).

Dynamics should become a part of your practice routine. By practicing a beat or drum roll at different volume levels, you will be able to control dynamics skillfully and incorporate it into your musical vocabulary.

It is worth practicing different dynamic levels. Experiment with the height of your stick and notice the differences in volume and attack that you can achieve across a wide dynamic range.

As you will discover, dynamics are an essential tool kit in the drummer's creative armory.

Above: High sticking position, sometimes referred to as a "full" stroke.

Above: A medium height sticking position.

Above: The low sticking position, also known as the "tap" stroke.

Left: Nirvana are known for their loud and heavy gigs, but here they can be seen playing in an acoustic situation for MTV's Unplugged series. Despite this quieter setting, dynamics still play a vital role.

Quarters, Eighths, and Sixteenths

We will now look at reading our first rhythm. Work through the following examples slowly until you are comfortable with them. You can either strike your snare drum or clap your hands to keep time. Each successive example introduces a new note value—the result is a mixture of notes and rests of varying lengths.

Above the stave is written the count, which you should say out loud: "1,2,3,4, 1,2,3,4" and so on. This gives you your time or "pulse." Tap out the notes with your hands and pay close attention to the different note lengths.

Look out for the repeat signs in figures 7, 8, and 9.

Below: Be sure to dedicate plenty of time to practicing new ideas.

Quarter Notes

Figure 1

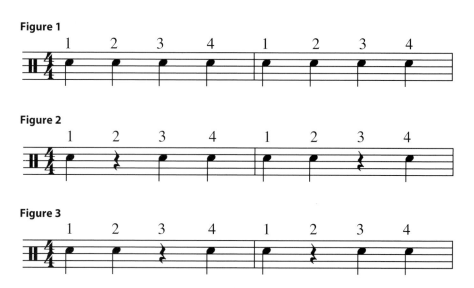

Figure 2

Figure 3

Eighth Notes

Here the counting is a little different from counting quarter notes. There is now a "+" between the numbers. You can practice counting it as "1 and, 2 and, 3 and, 4 and."

Figure 4

Figure 5

Figure 6

Sixteenth Notes

With sixteenth notes, we will be adding twice as many notes into the same bar length. Previously we have been counting 1 and 2 and 3 and 4 and, or 1 + 2 + 3 + 4 +. With sixteenth notes we need to change the way we count. Note: The length of the bar will not change, but we will be playing 16 notes overall, instead of 8. To count sixteenths, we will use the following counting method:

1 e + a 2 e + a 3 e + a 4 e + a

So, when spoken out loud, this would sound like—one—ee—and—a—two—ee—and—a—three—ee—and—a—four—ee—and—a.

You will also notice that the notes are grouped (or beamed) into groups of four. This makes them easier to read. Unlike the eighth notes, which have a single beam, the sixteenth notes have a double beam. When you see this, you know you are dealing with sixteenth notes.

By counting in this way, we can add more notes into the same period of time. This means that sixteenth notes don't take twice as long to play, but that they are played in the same amount of time as the eighth notes.

Above: Daily practice is essential, both for those just starting to learn and also for seasoned professionals.

Figure 7

Figure 8

Figure 9

About Triplets

On the previous pages we looked at simple rhythms in 4/4, which are easily divisible by four. Sometimes, however, there will be a need to play in "three," or triplets. This creates a different character to the rhythm, but we want to keep the time signature the same—4/4. Below we will discover how this is done.

This is possible by using triplets (three notes), where three beats are squeezed into a count of one. The example below shows how this works. The shuffle groove that we will look at later on also uses triplets to give it its distinctive feel.

In Figure 1, right, you can see that there are four groups of beamed notes. Each group has three notes. These are triplets. We can count these out in the following way:

1 + a 2 + a 3 + a 4 + a

When spoken out loud this would sound like— "one—and—a—two—and—a—three—and— a—four—and—a."

To get an idea of the triplet feel, on counts 1, 2, 3, and 4 hit the drum a little harder (this creates an accent, or louder note). Here's the count again, but the numbers in bold mean that you should play a louder note. While doing this you should also be counting out loud, so say the bold numbers more loudly as well.

1 + a **2** + a **3** + a **4** + a

This should give you an idea of how the triplet sounds.

If you add up all these counts, you get 12—the same number as all the beamed notes added together. We can divide these 12 notes by three—which gives us four (this represents the four counts to the bar, and for every count we can play three notes).

Grouping triplets in this way within a 4/4 framework is often referred to as artificial grouping.

Don't get confused with 3/4, in which there are three notes to every bar. The triplets work within a 4/4 time signature because we are still going to count four beats to the bar (as opposed to three notes in 3/4). The difference here is that for every beat we are going to fit in three notes. In the example below three notes will be played.

Figure 1

1 + a 2 + a 3 + a 4 + a

Left: For a good example of a triplet groove, listen to Fats Domino's "Blueberry Hill" from 1956. Many songs of this era make use of triplet and shuffle grooves and were very popular in the rhythm and blues music of the day.

As with all the exercises in this book, start slowly when you try to tap out these rhythms, then build up your speed as your confidence increases. However, drumming isn't just about playing as fast as you can: sometimes playing at slow tempos can be deceptively tricky. This is because the spaces between the notes are greater and any mistakes really stand out!

Here are two more for you to try:

Figure 2

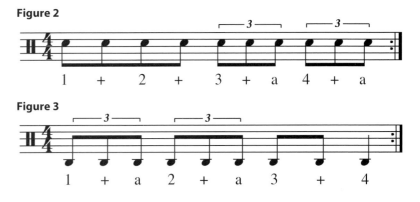

Figure 3

COMPOUND TIME
When we play music that uses triplets in its composition, it is formally referred to as "compound time." When we play in 4/4, we call it common time. Time signatures, such as 6/8 and 9/8, are made up from groups of three note clusters, or triplets. 6/8, for example, can be called a compound duple meter because it is divided into equal parts—that is, two sets of three notes that equal six overall.

Left: Triplets are an essential part of the drummer's vocabulary and can be applied to any part of the drum set.

Grip and Posture

Drumstick grips and posture are both very important to the drummer. By getting these basics right, you will be able to progress further and develop your playing career. Some beginners may overlook this and consequently struggle to achieve their goals until they finally get it right. There are two main grips to use, and it is up to you which you prefer.

It is worth spending some time becoming accustomed to these drumstick grips during your early practice sessions.

Traditional Grip

This style of grip originated in military drumming and it has since become popular with modern drummers. The right hand holds the stick as in the matched grip (shown below), while the left hand holds the stick between the third and second finger with the butt resting between the thumb and first finger. If you are left-handed, then naturally, you would hold the sticks in the opposite hands.

Matched Grip

This is the most commonly used grip and developed from orchestral percussion playing. There are three styles: German, American, and French, although you may use a mixture of all three while playing. The stick is held between the index finger and the thumb with the remaining fingers curled underneath. It is essential not to grip too tightly.

Left: The traditional grip.

Left: German matched grip—palm facing down.

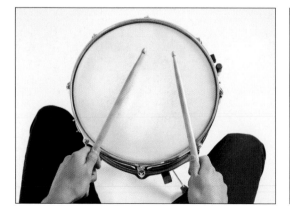

Left: French matched grip—palm facing inward.

Far left: American matched grip—palm between the other two positions at 45°.

Finding the Balance Point

It is important to find the balance point or fulcrum of the stick. Once found, the stick pivots in a natural way. This creates a responsive bounce from the drumheads.

Rest the butt end of the stick on your index finger. Lift the tip end and let it drop on the snare drum and you will see that it doesn't bounce particularly well. Try again, but rest the stick halfway up. Experiment with the points between to find the best bounce.

Above: Start by holding the stick at its base (fattest end) and rest it on your index finger.

Above: Now raise the stick and then let it drop onto the snare to see how it bounces.

Above: Repeat this process but hold the stick almost midway. You should notice a better bounce.

Posture

There are no hard and fast rules concerning your posture. Every person's body is a different shape, so my recommendations may not be right for you. But it's worth experimenting until you are completely comfortable when sitting at your kit. However, the following points will be useful to adhere to:

Make sure that you sit upright and that you set the height of your drum throne so that your thighs are angled slightly downward.

Your elbows should hang by your side, and your arms should be held slightly away from the body as if you were holding an egg in each armpit. Be careful to keep your shoulders completely relaxed at all times.

Control the stick movement from your wrist and not with your whole arm.

Any tension in your shoulders or in your arms will create resistance. This will make it harder to play and you will tire more quickly. Drumming shouldn't be a strain. The drums play you as much as you play them!

For a right-handed player, your right hand plays the hi-hat, under which your left hand will play the snare drum. Your right foot should be on the bass drum pedal, and your left on the hi-hat pedal (which controls the opening and closing of the hats). If you are left-handed, then just reverse the kit.

Above: Good posture is important, not only for your general well-being but also because it affects your ability to play fluently. Notice the straight back and relaxed shoulders.

Strokes

Strokes enable you to play dynamic sounds. As with all the exercises in this book, you should make them a part of your everyday practice. Mastering these will give you greater control over your drumming skills.

There are four strokes for you to get to grips with. The tap stroke, the full stroke, the up stroke, and the down stroke.

Tap Stroke (T)
Both sticks should be in a low position. Because of this, the tap creates softer "ghost" notes.

Right: Tap stroke 1.

Far right: Tap stroke 2.

Full Stroke (F)
Here the stroke begins at a higher position and as a consequence creates a louder "accent" stroke.

Right: Full stroke 1.

Far right: Full stroke 2.

Up Stroke (U)

Start in the low position and play a ghost note, then lift the stick to the high position in readiness to make an accented stroke.

Right: Up stroke 1.

Far right: Up stroke 2.

Down Stroke (D)

Start in the high position and play an accented note. End in a low position as if about to play a ghost note.

Right: Down stroke 1.

Far right: Down stroke 2.

If you have managed to grasp all the basic knowledge and skills outlined in this chapter, you will now be ready to look at applying these ideas in practicality.

In the following chapter we will look at the rudiments, which form the basis of all drumming.

Left: If you master the basics, you will soon be competent enough to play with other musicians.

Chapter 3

Rudiments

When learning the guitar or piano, you will have to learn and practice scales in which you run through the notes that make up the octave of any scale in ascending or descending order. In drumming there aren't scales as such, but something called rudiments. These exercises introduce various roll exercises that will become your fills, or "chops." Officially there are 40 rudiments in total, but we will look at arguably the most useful to establish some basic skills to get you started.

The Building Blocks for Your Chops

As mentioned previously, modern drumming can trace its origins back to the military. The rudiments were developed not only as a form of music but also as a language to direct the movement of troops on the battlefield. Today this is no longer necessary, but the skills have been passed down and adopted by drummers all around the world.

If you have ever seen (or heard) a military snare drummer, you will have witnessed someone with a complete mastery of the rudiments (you may have also noticed their use of the traditional grip, by the way).

Rudiments are the single most important part of drumming—in many ways, they are drumming. All the beats and grooves you will play utilize the rudiments in some form or other.

Initially 26 rudiments were set down by the National Association of Rudimental Drummers, or NARD, which was formed in 1933 by a group of drummers in Chicago. These are commonly known as the 26 American rudiments. As time has gone by, more rudiments have appeared as set out by the Percussive Arts Society, or PAS. These now include 40 rudiment patterns (the international rudiments) from all over the world.

It is up to you whether you want to learn them all, but for the time being it is useful to learn a few essential patterns to get you going. Perfecting them will improve your overall technique and control and may even inspire you to create your own. Drumming after all is a language and it is in your power to develop your own distinctive vocabulary within this language.

As with all these exercises, it is always a good idea to use a metronome and practice using different tempos. But don't try to play too fast initially—start slowly and build up your control over time.

The importance of the rudiments cannot be overstressed. To a beginner, the exercises may seem a little unexciting—even boring—but without mastering them your drumming skills will always be limited. A little practice each day will, over time, pay rich dividends.

RUDIMENT FACTS

Beyond the official 40 rudiments there are many so-called "hybrid" rudiments with bizarre names such as "the herta," "walt-diddles," and "nuttchada." They are often referred to as informal rudiments because they fall outside the accepted rudiments. They are described as hybrid rudiments because they combine two or more standard rudiments together. For example, if you add a paradiddle to a flam, it might be called a paraflam, or perhaps a paraflamadiddle. There are hundreds of hybrids out there, with many Web sites dedicated to them. You might want to create a few of your own!

Above: *A line of military drummers. Many hours of practicing rudiments enable them to play complex parts in perfect unison.*

DAILY RUDIMENT WORKOUT

A good way to approach rudiment practice is to set up a structured regime. This way you can monitor your progress. You can spend as much time as you like doing this—10 minutes is good, but so is several hours! It's up to you.

Firstly, decide which rudiment you want to focus on, or you may decide to practice a combination.

Set your metronome to the desired tempo. It is better to practice at slower bpms (beats per minute). Try 70 bpm to begin with—although the ability to play at 40 bpm is worth achieving. As you improve, you can then increase the tempo.

It is also of value to practice rudiments without a metronome. By doing this you can start slowly and increase the speed and then slow down again.

You Will Need

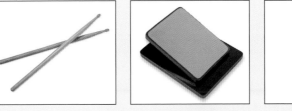

Pair of drumsticks   **Practice pad/drum set**   **Metronome**

Remember to keep a count going in your head, or if it helps, to say the count out loud.

Rudiment practice shouldn't be a chore. If you feel bored to begin with, think of them as you would about having driving lessons—once you have mastered the basic skills, you can obtain your license to drive wherever you want!

Below: It is worth practicing your rudiments on the snare drum, or a practice pad. Eventually they can be applied to all parts of the drum set.

Single Stroke Rolls

Single stroke rolls are number one on the rudiment list. They form the basis for all the other rudiments that you will learn. You will be able to play these straight away, but pay close attention to the spacing between the notes. Don't go too fast initially. Using a metronome will help greatly to maintain the rhythm.

The main thing here is to remain completely relaxed and try not to grip the sticks tightly. A loose but balanced relationship between the hand, stick, and bounce is crucial for effective execution.

You must also get used to the idea of using your remaining fingers that are curled under the stick to exert control over the stroke. By lightly "flicking" the stick with these fingers, you will, with practice, be able to bounce the stick at its fulcrum. You will notice how the stick then does all the work for you without any need for excessive force from your wrist or arm.

Left: Aim for evenly spaced and accurate strokes as you practice this rudiment.

As soon as you feel any tension growing because you are trying to play too fast, stop, take a couple of breaths, and begin again.

Here are a few single stroke roll exercises for you to practice. For now, just play them on the snare or practice pad, but they can be played on any part of the kit to create interesting musical phrases.

You can see from these examples how important it is to switch the sticking from left to right and back again. To achieve an equal balance between left and right is the goal. If you are right handed, you may feel that your left hand is "weaker" or less dextrous. This is natural, but with perseverance you will improve your technique with your weaker hand.

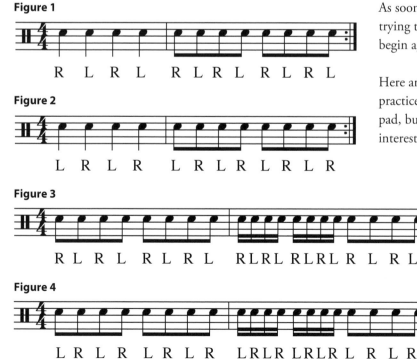

Figure 1

R L R L R L R L R L R L

Figure 2

L R L R L R L R L R L R

Figure 3

R L R L R L R L RLRL RLRL R L R L

Figure 4

L R L R L R L R LRLR LRLR L R L R

SINGLE STROKE STICKING

Normally you would use your wrist to articulate the stroke. Another way to play the stroke is using the bounce technique. This can, once mastered, greatly increase the speed of your rolls.

Let the stick bounce back up to the start position.

Repeat these three steps until you achieve an even bounce. Now try applying this technique to the exercises opposite.

Below: You can apply the single stroke roll all round the kit. By mastering this, you will be able to perform exciting rolls and fills.

Position the stick at around 45 degrees above the snare. Hold the stick in the matched grip style between the index finger and thumb. Keep the remaining fingers loose.

With the remaining three fingers lightly flick the underside of the stick, which should cause it to strike the snare head.

Double Stroke Rolls and Variations

The double stroke roll is another rudiment that you will often come across.
This can seem tricky at first, but with perseverance you should develop a smooth and
effective roll. You will be striking the drum twice with your right stick, then twice with
your left stick, and so on.

Once again let the fulcrum method do all the work for you and try not to play these rolls too fast initially. What we're looking for here are even, well-executed strokes.

Figure 1

R R L L   R R L L R R L L

Start very slowly and then gradually work up the speed of the roll to your current maximum speed, then slow down again.

Figure 2

L L R R   L L R R L L R R

These next rolls are extensions from the double stroke roll and are worth memorizing so that they can be incorporated into your playing.

Note how the final, primary stroke is accented. These strokes sound best when played quickly, but don't try this straight away. Start slowly and build up your speed. It is more important that the notes sound good and are played with a confident, controlled execution. Notice the accents in the examples.

The three examples, below, use a combination of eighth, sixteenth, and thirty-second notes. Thirty-second notes are twice as fast as sixteenth notes. In this context they help to suggest how fast these rolls can be played when up to speed, but as with any aspect of practice, play these slowly at first.

Above: With double strokes we can begin to use the bounce of the drum to create impressive-sounding rolls.

Five Stroke Roll

RRLLR

Six Stroke Roll

RLLRRL

Seven Stroke Roll

RRLLRRL

DOUBLE STROKE STICKING

As with the single stroke roll, you can utilize the bounce sticking technique to increase speed.

Position the stick at around 45 degrees above the snare. Hold the stick in the matched grip style between the index finger and thumb. Keep the remaining fingers loose.

With the remaining three fingers, lightly flick the underside of the stick, which should cause it to strike the snare head. The difference here from single bounce sticking is that the stick should bounce twice before returning to the start position.

Let the stick bounce back up to the start position.

This can be tricky to master initially and sometimes you may get three notes, or more. To help this, try the "drop and hold" method. When the stick returns to the start position close the three "loose" fingers around the stick (don't grip too tightly.) Some players try different matched grips to improve their double technique.

Below: Every rhythm you play will be based on a rudiment.

The Diddle

Diddle rudiments are combinations of single and double strokes played in a particular pattern. When combined with accents, they become particularly effective as musical phrases when applied to the kit.

Paradiddles

No one really knows the origin of the name paradiddle, although the first mention of it can be dated to the 1920s. It is certain that a form of the paradiddle was played many, many years before and it probably dates back to the 17th century. The paradiddle is one of the most important and useful rudiments for a drummer to learn. In fact, it is essential that you learn it because it can be used to create distinctive fills and grooves around the set. There are many forms of the "diddle" to master, but to start with we will get to know three: the single paradiddle, the double paradiddle, and the paradiddle-diddle.

When beginning to learn these rudiments, you may find the sticking order initially confusing. They have a specific order and there are also stroke instructions to consider. This may seem confusing at first, but in fact they are very useful in the long run because they enable you to execute the patterns accurately and effectively.

There is some disagreement regarding the best method of practicing these rudiments. Some commentators advocate the use of a metronome. By using a metronome, you can practice to a steady unchanging tempo. The benefit of this is that you can develop very accurate and controlled diddles. Others advise you not to use a metronome, but in fact to begin the diddle slowly, and then increase the tempo gradually to as fast as you can comfortably play, then decrease the tempo. The obvious advantage to this is that you develop control through tempo changes. The answer, of course, is to use both techniques. Practicing any aspect of your drumming to a metronome has no real downsides. Remember, good timekeeping is the prerequisite of any drummer worth his salt. But there is also great value to practicing without one, because you can develop the ability to play smooth and accurate tempo transitions.

Below: The paradiddle is a versatile rudiment that can be used in fills and also to create interesting grooves.

When reading these examples, look out for the accents and also the stroke instructions. Remember, T equals tap stroke, F equals full stroke, U equals up stroke, D equals down stroke.

Single Paradiddle

The notation (right) shows the classic paradiddle rudiment. Broken down it consists of two (alternating) single strokes that are followed by a double stroke: Right, Left, Right—Right, and then it swaps over—Left, Right, Left—Left. Or R L R R, L R L L.

Note that in this example the notes are sixteenth notes (because of the double-beamed groups). This doesn't mean that they have to be played as sixteenths, however.

Underneath we have the sticking-order instructions as described above. Below these are the stroke instructions. These are described in more detail on pages 34 and 35, but to summarize we have "D"—down stroke, "U"—up stroke, and "T"—the tap stroke.

On the first note of each grouping of four notes there is also an accent symbol. This means that this note should be played louder than the following three notes.

Double Paradiddle

The double paradiddle is a triplet-based rudiment, meaning that it is divided into groups of three. The first group consists of three alternating single strokes: Right, Left, Right. The next group has a single stroke followed by a double stroke: Left, Right—Right. It then swaps over: Left, Right, Left (third group), Right, Left—Left (fourth group). Or R L R L RR, L R L R LL.

The stroke instructions contain Down, Up, and Tap strokes, but there is also a new stroke: F—full stroke, which occurs on the first note of groups 1 and 3.

In groups 1 and 3 there are also two accents to play, on beats one and three of each respective group.

Paradiddle-diddle

In this third example of a diddle rudiment, the wonderfully named paradiddle-diddle, we can see another group of triplets. It looks deceptively like

Single Paradiddle

R	L	R	R	L	R	L	L	R	L	R	R	L	R	L	L
D	U	T	T	D	U	T	T	D	U	T	T	D	U	T	T

Double Paradiddle

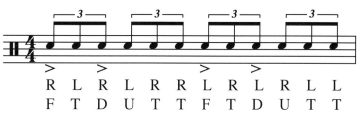

R	L	R	L	R	R	L	R	L	R	L	L
F	T	D	U	T	T	F	T	D	U	T	T

Paradiddle-diddle

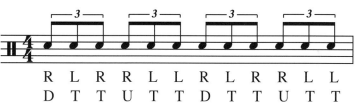

R	L	R	R	L	L	R	L	R	R	L	L
D	T	T	U	T	T	D	T	T	U	T	T

the double paradiddle, but look carefully—it's not the same.

Note the sticking order: R L R R LL, R L R R LL. The stroke instructions also differ from the previous diddle—there is no full stroke: D T T U TT, D T T U TT. There are no accents to worry about either!

Try each example until you feel confident, and perhaps even memorize them. If you have a metronome, then practice them individually until you can play them at around 90 beats per minute (90 bpm).

Once you have achieved this, then play all three as a group, one after another: start with the single paradiddle, followed by the double paradiddle, and finish up with the paradiddle-diddle, as if it was one piece. You should notice over time that they improve your technique greatly. You will also notice that you have a weaker hand: if you are right handed, your weak hand will usually be your left and vice-versa. Practicing the diddles will help to strengthen your weak hand.

Above: Always start slowly and build up to the next tempo when you are ready.

Flams

Although it may sound like some sort of pastry dish, the flam is actually a deceptively tricky rudiment. When played well it gives the drummer a new and distinctive sound, which can liven up more standard-sounding rolls, as we will see.

Essentially, the flam rudiment consists of a quieter, ghost note, which is followed by a louder accented note. Look at the example below:

The Standard Flam

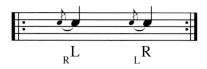

This is the standard flam. Looks simple, doesn't it? But if you look more closely, what actually appear to be two notes are, in fact, four. We have two quarter notes preceded by smaller eighth notes. These smaller notes are called ghost notes.

The "space" between the notes, or the length of counted time is hard to write down. This is because it is not actually counted. When played correctly, it will give the impression of an "augmented" note, or longer note. The ghost note ornaments the louder "primary" note.

Initially you may struggle to get a good flam sound, but there is a specific sticking technique, which should guarantee perfect flams every time--see the three easy steps, right:

Left: Place your right hand in the tap (T) position.

Left: Then place your left hand in the full (F) position.

Left: Now, just let the sticks drop to the surface of the snare.

You have just executed a perfect standard flam!

Using the technique described practice until you achieve even, controlled flams. In The Standard Flam (on the previous page) the flams alternate—the first flam has a left ghost note followed by a right primary note, then it flips over: a right ghost note followed by a left primary note. As with the diddle rudiments on the previous page, you may find that your weaker hand is causing you trouble. If you are right-handed, you may find the second flam easier than the first, but don't over-practice what you find easier to do. One of the main purposes of practicing is to discover where your weak areas lie, to pinpoint them. Once you have done this, you can target these areas for special attention. There really is no point in practicing something you can already do at the expense of something you can't!

After achieving a good sounding flam, reach for the metronome and practice them to various tempos. Count "1, 2, 3, 4" and on every count execute a flam—remember to alternate them so that your technique develops in a balanced way. Try these tempos to begin with: 60 bpm, 80 bpm, and 110 bpm.

Flam Accent

The flam accent is a triplet-based flam. Here we have two groups of three note patterns with each group beginning with a flam and followed by two single strokes. Here, the initial primary note in both groups is accented, so play this note louder than the next two notes. If it helps, count "1,2,3, 1,2,3" out loud.

Again, this pattern can appear to be deceptively simple. You have to watch out for the alternating sticking and initially you may find this rudiment frustrating. However, start slowly. Play it through until you start to feel more comfortable. When learning these unfamiliar patterns, your brain will be doing all the work, but once you become more

accustomed, then you will find that you "think" less about them, and that, in fact, your hands do all the work for you.

Flam Tap

Here we have a flam pattern based on two groups of four notes, which in this example are written as sixteenth notes. Take a look at the sticking: what we appear to have here is a double stroke roll—R R L L, R R L L. To make this a flam rudiment and not just a double stroke roll, two ghost notes have been added within each group of four. There is a ghost note preceding the first and third notes of each group. To complicate matters, there are also accent marks placed on the primary notes (notes 1 and 3).

Remember to stay relaxed: You may start "snatching," become tense and try to force the flams into existence. As soon as this becomes apparent, stop. Nothing can be gained from playing this way. Keep your shoulders relaxed, play from the wrists and fulcrum (the balancing point of the sticks). Some find it useful to sway their bodies from side to side when trying these examples. If using a metronome, don't set it too fast and, above all, don't be dismayed if you think you're not making progress. You are. The very act of practicing means that you are improving every moment.

Above: A Latin percussionist performs at a festival. Latin rhythms, such as the samba, incorporate various rudiments, including the flam, to create a unique and exciting sound.

RUDIMENT RHYTHMS
The most important thing to remember is that these rudiments shouldn't just be brainteasers— they are, in fact, meant to be rhythms first and foremost. When attempting these for the first time, this may not seem the case, but gradually as you become more adept you will start to hear, and enjoy, these patterns more.

Drags

Drag rudiments are made up from two quieter ghost notes followed by a louder stroke, which is referred to as the primary stroke. The ghost notes are played by one hand and the primary note by the other.

Like the flam, it is hard to convey accurately the space between the ghost notes. However, they are played extremely close together, but not so close as to be smothered by the primary note. The double ghost notes should be played at twice the speed of the context that they are in. If the passage happens to be a sixteenth note sequence, then the drag ghost notes should be played as if they are thirty-second notes.

The Drag

The two preceding ghost notes should be played quickly and more softly than the primary note that follows them. Try playing the ghost notes with your left, and the primary note with your right: LL **R**. Then reverse the sticking thus: RR **L**.

The Single Drag Tap

For this type of drag, try the following sticking: LL **R L**, then follow that with RR **L R**.

These can come in very useful when you are creating fills (see Chapter 6). For example, play a single stroke roll followed by a drag or even a single drag tap. Rudiments aren't meant to be played in isolation—they start to become a lot of fun when put together in various combinations.

There are a plethora of drag rudiments for you to try. Below are some more drags of increasing complexity for you to practice.

Double Drag Tap

Single Ratamacue

Double Ratamacue

Triple Ratamacue

As you can see, many of the more advanced drags combine other rudiments, such as the paradiddle. This small selection should keep you occupied for some time!

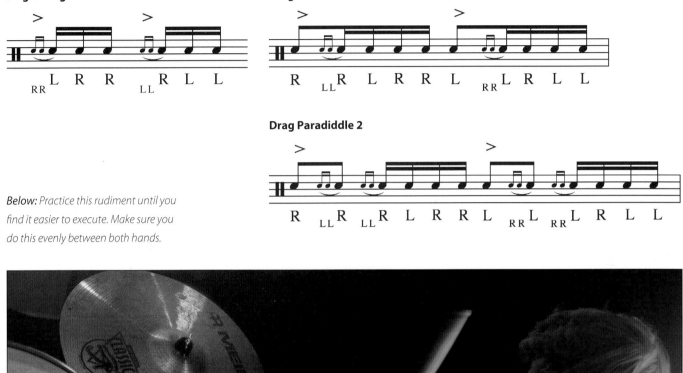

Single Dragadiddle

R R L R R L L R L L

Drag Paradiddle 1

R L L R L R R L R R L R L L

Drag Paradiddle 2

R L L R L L R L R R L R R R L L R L R L L L

Below: Practice this rudiment until you find it easier to execute. Make sure you do this evenly between both hands.

Multiple Bounce Roll

If you have ever visited the circus, you may have noticed a drummer, sometimes a clown, standing with a large snare drum upon which he plays a long "buzzing" roll that usually ends with a cymbal crash. This is the multiple bounce roll, sometimes referred to as a buzz roll. It is an important rudiment in the drummer's armory.

One way to describe the multiple bounce roll, or "buzz," is to imagine it is a single stroke roll with an unspecified number of quieter bounces in between. It is a good idea to practice this roll quietly and build up to a crescendo and then go back down again (decrescendo). Play the roll on the snare and move around the surface of the head. Note the different tonal textures as your sticks travel.

When written down in notation form, the buzz looks like this:

The example opposite gives an idea of a buzz roll played in context with a simple beat, which for the sake of demonstration is played on the floor tom.

Right: The multiple bounce roll can be used as a great fill.

Below: Experiment with playing on all areas of the snare head to achieve different tonal textures.

Multiple Bounce Roll number 1

It is also important to use either a metronome to try this at different speeds or to count out loud, or in your head, otherwise the roll will become formless. As you improve, you might want to try inserting accented notes at your own prescribed intervals, or randomly. Give yourself a set length—maybe a count of 8, 16, or 32 within which to execute the buzz.

Great examples of the buzz roll can be heard in most jazz drumming because its delicate nature lends itself well to that subtle form of music, although not exclusively so. Buzz rolls can also be used effectively as introductions and endings to songs.

Here are some more examples of the multiple bounce roll for you to try:

Left: Jazz drummer Max Roach, who pioneered the jazz style of bebop, used the multiple bounce roll effectively in his playing.

Below: Multiple bounce rolls are often played on the snare drum, but can be applied to any part of the drum set.

Multiple Bounce Roll number 2

Multiple Bounce Roll number 3

In addition to the standard multiple bounce roll, there is also the triple stroke roll. As the name suggests, it uses triplets in its structure. There are three strokes per hand—RRR LLL.

For the most effective execution of this roll, you should use the bounce stroke method as described previously for single and double stroke rolls. The difference, of course, is that you must allow the stick to bounce three times.

Triple Stroke Roll

R R R L L L R R R L L L

Chapter 4
Your First Beat

In the previous chapter we spent some time learning about the rudiments of drumming, but that is only the beginning. As a drummer you will want to play "beats" or "grooves." The rudiments should be practiced in tandem with these beats. As you improve, you will incorporate the rudiments within the beats. These become the basis for your "fills" (which we will look at later) and beat construction. But before all that, we will look at your first beat, an eighth note feel beat.

The Eighth Note Beat—1

Here we will construct our first groove, an eighth note feel beat in 4/4. This beat is so called because it contains eight notes. It is sometimes known as the basic rock beat and is the staple of many classic songs, including Michael Jackson's "Billie Jean."

The following examples all assume that you are a right-handed drummer. If you happen to be left-orientated, then you simply swap everything over.

The hi-hat should be played with your right hand over your left, which takes care of the snare. Your right foot controls the bass drum. Your left foot should be firmly on the hi-hat pedal so that the hats are closed.

Parts of the Kit Used

Hi-Hat

Snare Drum

Bass Drum

THE BACKBEAT

When you hear this type of groove being played, either by a live drummer or on record, you can identify it as a "backbeat" groove. This is so called because the snare drum is played on beats two and four of the bar.

The origins of this phrase go back to the early days of drum development in New Orleans. The drummer Fred Maddox became famous at this time for his backbeat groove, which he is believed to have played as far back as 1937. This groove evolved over time into rockabilly music and then rock and roll, as made famous on tunes performed by Elvis Presley and The Beatles early in their career.

Because of its simple, yet hypnotic, metronomic feel (it's particularly easy to dance to), it has become the basis for the vast majority of contemporary pop and rock tunes.

Right: Before you start, make sure you are sitting in the correct position at the drum set.

Eighth Note with Hi-Hat

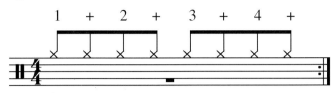

Now we introduce the bass drum on beats 1 and 3. Be careful to make sure the bass drum and hi-hat notes are played in unison. By unison, I mean that they are played together—at exactly the same time. If either note is played a fraction before, or after, the other, then you will get a messy, smudged sound.

Here we go. In this example we will just play the hi-hat. Note the counting instructions above the stave—"1 + 2 + 3 + 4 +". The hi-hat notes fall on the number as well as the "+." It is helpful to count the pulse out loud.

Eighth Note with Hi-Hat and Bass Drum

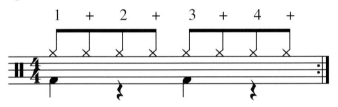

The next stage is to introduce a third element—the snare drum on beats 2 and 4.

Eighth Note with Hi-Hat, Snare, and Bass Drum

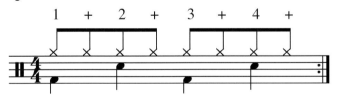

There you have it—your first beat! Keep practicing this until you get an even and smooth groove going. When you get more confident, why not set up a metronome and try playing in time to it? Try different tempos, but don't go too fast!

Above: The hi-hat acts as the "pulse" through the groove.

Above: The snare drum is the focal point of much of your playing. This creates the "backbeat" (see opposite).

Above: The bass drum "anchors" down your groove and creates a low counterpoint to the snare.

The Eighth Note Beat—2

These following examples introduce different bass drum patterns within the eighth note beat. The placement of the bass drum can dramatically alter the overall character of the beat, as we will discover. By adding or moving the bass drum, a simple beat can be transformed.

In some ways, playing the drums can be likened to driving a car. All four of your limbs are being asked to carry out independent movements. As a beginner you may find that your limbs just won't do what you are asking them to do! This is a common problem. Don't lose heart though. Over time, the muscles in your arms and legs will build up "muscle memory" and obey the separate orders being given to them by your brain. Try each example slowly and remember to count out loud.

Parts of the Kit Used

Hi-Hat

Snare Drum

Bass Drum

Eighth Note Alternate Bass Drum number 1

In this example an extra bass drum event has been added at the "+" after beat 3.

Eighth Note Alternate Bass Drum number 2

In this example a new bass drum note has been added to the "+" after beat 1.

Eighth Note Alternate Bass Drum number 3

Notice here how the bass drum note has moved to the "+" after beat 2.

Eighth Note Alternate Bass Drum number 4

Watch out for beat 3—there is no bass drum here. Attempt this slowly at first until you "get" the groove!

BASS DRUM TECHNIQUE

Unsurprisingly, there are many ways that you can approach playing the bass drum. It is incredibly important that you spend some time developing the technique that is right for you. As with all drumming, you must be able to perform accurate bass drum notes. Some players go for speed (double bass drum pedals are popular with many heavy metal drummers), but all must attain control, independence, and accuracy. Below are three techniques for you to experiment with. Again, there is no right or wrong way—if your chosen technique works for you, then that's what you should go for.

Heel-Up Method

As the name suggests, you raise your heel and then strike the pedal with the ball of your foot. Your toes should rest lightly on the pedal.

Right: Heel up.
Far right: Heel down.

Heel-Down Method

Keep your heel resting on the pedal plate, then raise your toes and strike the pedal with them. This method is popular with jazz drummers, because it creates a softer, more controlled note.

Right: Start position.
Far right: Toe down.

Heel-Toe Method

This method is trickier to master, but can enable you to play fast bass drum notes. It is an amalgam of the two previous techniques.

Raise your heel.

Bring the heel down to strike the pedal while lifting your toes.

Strike with your toes and lift your heel.

The Eighth Note Beat—3

Having looked at bass drum variations, we now look at placing the snare drum at different points within the beat. The hi-hat with its trebly, high sound remains a constant throughout—this acts as an "anchor" for the beat. It ties the bass drum (low part) and the snare drum (mid part) together.

By altering the position of the snare drum, we can create some very different-sounding variations of the eighth note feel beat. The aim here, as with the previous examples, is to achieve an even character to the pattern.

Parts of the Kit Used

Hi-Hat

Snare Drum

Bass Drum

Eighth Note Alternate Snare number 1

The bass drum has returned to beats 1 and 3, but a new snare event has been added.

Eighth Note Alternate Snare number 2

Another variation with two extra snare beats.

Eighth Note Alternate Snare number 3

Only three snare events here. Their placement creates a very different sounding beat.

Eighth Note Alternate Snare number 4

The fourth variation—with a different placement of the snare events.

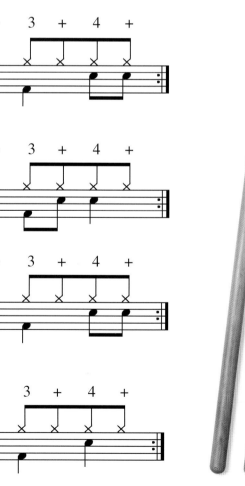

THE RIMSHOT

Normally when striking the snare drum, you should aim for the center of the drum—you can tell a professional drummer from a beginner because the center of his drumheads are usually marked (where the stick hits) around this area. The snare drum is capable of creating many sounds depending on where and how you hit it. If you strike near the edge of the head, it will create a tone with a distinct "ring." In the center it becomes shorter and tighter in character. One snare striking technique you may want to try is the rimshot. The Yes and King Crimson drummer Bill Bruford is famed for his use of the snare rimshot. To execute this stroke:

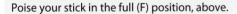

Poise your stick in the full (F) position, above.

Strike down toward the snare. At the point of contact the stick must strike the metal "rim" of the drum and the center of the head at the same time.

This close-up image, left, shows how the tip of the stick strikes the center point of the drumhead and the halfway point of the stick strikes the metal rim.

After striking, lift the stick back to the full (F) position again. See photograph above left.

This effective stroke greatly increases the volume of the note and also adds a deeper, more substantial character to it. By striking at these two points, you are combining the center sound with its shorter note and the rim sound with its "ringing" color.

Chapter 5

Adding To The Beat

Having looked at some different variations of the eighth note feel beat, we're going to investigate the sixteenth note feel beat. This beat, as the name suggests, uses sixteenth notes that create a very different-sounding groove. Along with the eighth note feel beat, this pattern is also very popular in rock and pop music and forms the basis for many funk and disco tracks. The main difference between sixteenth grooves and eighth grooves can be found in the hi-hat pattern, as we will see...

Counting Sixteenths—1

This chapter introduces a different way of counting the beat, and the hi-hat will play more notes than it has in the previous examples. Sixteenth note grooves add a layer of complexity that is very popular in funk music, for instance. Again, by adding extra notes to the beat, we can achieve a very different-sounding groove.

In chapter two (pages 28—29), we looked at the different way sixteenths are counted. Instead of 1 + 2 + 3 + 4 + (one and two and three and four and) as used for eighth notes, we will use this count:

1 e + a 2 e + a 3 e + a 4 e + a

Phonetically this would sound like: One—ee—and—a—Two—ee—and—a—Three—ee—and—a—Four—ee—and—a.

For every sound there will be a note event. Remember also that the beamed sixteenth notes are joined by a double line, so that you know they are sixteenths. So, in this count of four we will be playing twice as many notes as the eighth note pattern, but in the same amount of time.

Let's have a look at how this works. We will be using just the hi-hat to start with. Make sure the hi-hat is closed (by depressing your left foot on the hi-hat pedal). Now mark out an even beat on the hi-hat.

Parts of the Kit Used

Hi-Hat

Snare Drum

Bass Drum

Sixteenth Hi-Hat

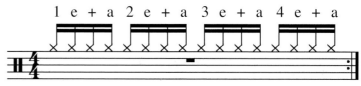

Each count represents a note played on the hi-hat (see notation above). This sets up the sixteenth note feel. Play this through a few times, and remember to count out loud. Once you are happy with your hi-hat groove, we can now start to construct the beat, starting with the bass drum.

Remember that it is important to keep counting through the pattern so that you are aware of where you are in the bar. Without this awareness you run the risk of becoming lost and the beat would then fall apart.

Now we can introduce the bass drum into the pattern.

Far left: Sixteenth note grooves can have an exciting visual impact when a drummer performs them on stage.

The bass drum occurs on beat 1 and beat 3 just as in the eighth note feel (see notation right). But the difference here is that you have doubled the number of hi-hat notes between the bass drum events by using sixteenth notes.

Sixteenth Hi-Hat and Bass Drum

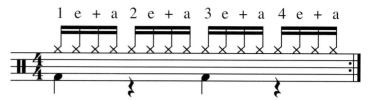

The snare drum notes are placed on beats 2 and 4 (see notation right). This placement of the snare is often referred to as the "backbeat."

Sixteenth Hi-Hat, Bass Drum, and Snare

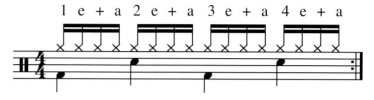

Again, take your time to develop the overall feel of the groove. Pull back the tempo if you start to feel any resistance or tension in your arms.

SOUNDS OF THE HI-HATS

Study of the hi-hat is worthy of a book on its own. There are many ways to play them and they are capable of creating many different sonic textures.

This can depend on where they are struck when they are closed or open. To find out for yourself, first strike the hats at the outer edge and slowly move toward the bell in the center. Now try the open style. This imparts a trashy character as the two separated cymbals crash against each other.

Other sounds can be created by open and closing the hats. For example, using your foot to open and close the hats (but not striking them with a stick) gives a pleasing "chick" sound which is often used in jazz drumming. If they are struck when being opened and closed, a longer, almost "slurping" sound is created.

Of course, drummers like to use variations of all of these, and sometimes all in one bar!

Above left: Closed hi-hat.

Above center: Open hi-hat.

Above right: Experiment when playing the hi-hat to appreciate the wide range of different sounds they are able to create.

Counting Sixteenths—2

We will now look at some more examples that require a larger contribution from the bass drum within the sixteenth note feel groove. Here the groove becomes decidedly more funky! Make sure to pay plenty of attention to your timing so that the beats "hold" together coherently.

You might find the sixteenth note pattern trickier to master than the eighth note. You will certainly find that there are some challenges to deal with once you start moving the bass drum around! But steady, unrushed practice will get you there. As with the previous examples, it is important to get the bass drum to fall in time with the hi-hat, otherwise you will notice how sloppy the beat sounds.

Parts of the Kit Used

Hi-Hat　　　　**Snare Drum**　　　　**Bass Drum**

Sixteenth Alternate Bass Drum number 1

As you can see there is a new bass drum note on the "+" of count 3.

Sixteenth Alternate Bass Drum number 2

Look out for the bass drum note on the "e" following count 4.

Sixteenth Alternate Bass Drum number 3

As you can see in this example, the bass drum note on beat one is a dotted note. What is a dotted note?

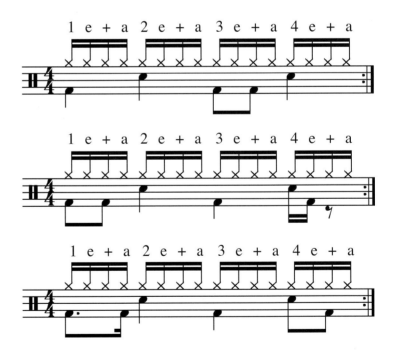

Dotted notes are used to describe notes longer than the normal note values. Normally this would mean that the note is worth half its value again.

For example, a whole note that is accompanied by a dot means that it is worth a count of 6 (a whole note is worth 4, half of 4 is 2. Added together we get 6). For instruments that can sustain their notes over different lengths of time, such as a piano or violin, this is not a problem, but for the drums this usually means something different. When you strike your bass drum, you will get one, short note—you can't make it sound any longer—you can't control its sustain.

In drum notation a dotted note will shift the placement of a following note. So, in the previous example, the bass drum on beat 1 is a dotted eighth note, which is worth 3/4 of a beat. This does not mean that you must try and play this beat for less than a count of 1—you can't do that, so don't try! It simply means the following bass drum note has shifted a beat forward (it now resides on the "a" in this group) and has become a sixteenth note.

Look at the table on the right to see how dotted notes and rests increase their value by one half of their value. Sixteenth dotted notes incidentally are rarely used and for now you don't need to worry about them.

Sixteenth Alternate Bass Drum number 4

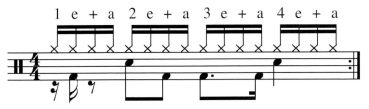

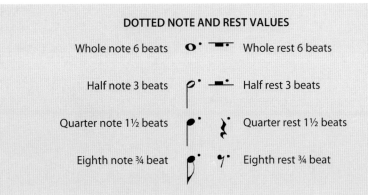

Make sure that you spot where the first bass drum appears! Not on the "1" but on the "e" immediately afterward.

DOTTED NOTE AND REST VALUES

Whole note 6 beats	○˙	━·	Whole rest 6 beats
Half note 3 beats	♩˙	▬·	Half rest 3 beats
Quarter note 1½ beats	♩˙	❭˙	Quarter rest 1½ beats
Eighth note ¾ beat	♪˙	♎˙	Eighth rest ¾ beat

Below: A drummer laying down a funky sixteenth groove.

Counting Sixteenths—3

It's time to move the snare drum around. In these examples the bass drum is solidly back on beats 1 and 3. Also introduced are what are known as "fills." These ornament your groove to create points of interest. You may notice how similar they are to some of the rudiments you practiced earlier.

Remember to check your posture—are your shoulders tense? Are you gripping the sticks too tightly? Always check to see if these things are as they should be. Remain conscious of how your body is feeling and try to stay relaxed and aware mentally. Mental tension can hinder your progress just as much as physical tension.

Parts of the Kit Used

Hi-Hat

Snare Drum

Bass Drum

Sixteenth Alternate Snare number 1

In this example an extra snare note has been added to the final "a" at the end of the measure. Play through this several times to loop the pattern.

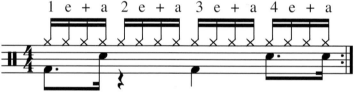

Crash Cymbal

Sixteenth Alternate Snare number 2

Here the snare doesn't fall where you might expect it. This creates a "syncopated" feel, meaning the snare's sixteenth-note events are "offset" from the main counts of 3 and 4.

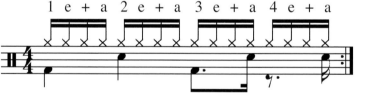

Tom-Toms

Sixteenth Alternate Snare number 3

There are two new parts of the kit that come into the equation here: the first tom (top space on the stave) and the floor tom (second space up above the bass drum line). The last section of this groove constitutes a "fill."

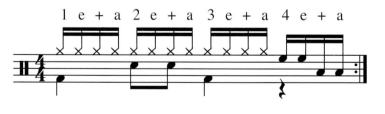

Sixteenth Alternate Snare number 4

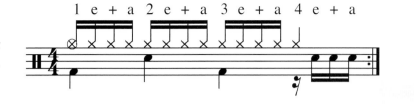

Note the cymbal crash at the beginning of the bar
and the fact that there is no hi-hat note on beat 1.
There are more fills for you to try in Chapter 6,
but feel free to experiment and make up your
own. When executing a fill always be aware of
where you start in the bar. If you place the fill
in the wrong section, it may sound a little odd.
For the time being, try to play a fill on beat 4 to
create some drama at the end of each bar.

*Below: As the beats become more advanced, you will have
the opportunity to play on other parts of the drum set.*

Chapter 6

Moving On

You now have some knowledge of notation theory, the rudiments and eighth and sixteenth beats. Armed with these skills, you have the opportunity to develop your drumming skills and extend your technique beyond the basics. In this final chapter we will look at some other interesting areas and end with a longer "final piece" for you to try.

Triplets and Shuffles

In the preceding two chapters we have looked at grooves that are easily divisible by two or four. Triplets, as their name suggests, are divisible by three. For more information on triplets refer back to pages 30—31—About Triplets.

Triplets

In the following three examples we're going to learn to count in threes in 4/4 time. As with eighths and sixteenths, we're going to start with the hi-hat and then add the remaining two elements, the bass drum and the snare.

Parts of the Kit Used

Hi-Hat

Snare Drum

Bass Drum

Triplet with Hi-Hat

Remember that we are using triplets here. We have 12 notes to play and for clarity they are grouped in threes, as marked. On the hi-hat count: 1 + a 2 + a 3+ a 4 + a, or "one—and—a—two—and—a—three—and—a—four—and—a." Once you are comfortable with this, we will then introduce the bass drum.

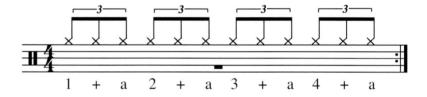

Triplet with Hi-Hat and Bass Drum

The counting remains the same as does the hi-hat pattern, but on the first beat of group 1 and 3 we will add a bass drum. Note the rests—they mean don't play the bass drum!

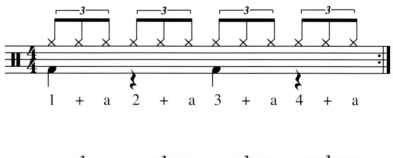

Triplet with Hi-Hat, Bass Drum, and Snare

To complete our first triplet groove, you must add the snare, which now replaces the rests in the previous step. Play this through until you are confident, and remember to keep counting out loud.

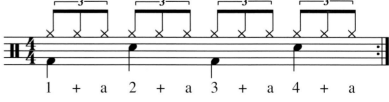

The Shuffle

The "shuffle" is another kind of triplet-based groove, which is commonly, but not exclusively, used in rhythm and blues music. Look at the following examples. As with the other grooves, we're going to build the shuffle from the hi-hat up.

Shuffle with Hi-Hat

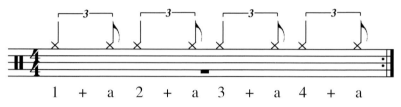

As you can see, the hi-hat is placed differently to the standard triplet. The count remains the same, but the hi-hat notes only occur on the first beat of each group and on the "a" of each group. Be careful not to play the hi-hat on the "+"!

Shuffle with Hi-Hat and Bass Drum

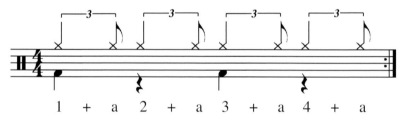

As with the standard triplet, the bass drum is placed on the first beat of group 1 and 3. Play this through several times until you can "loop" the pattern smoothly.

Shuffle with Hi-Hat, Bass Drum, and Snare Drum

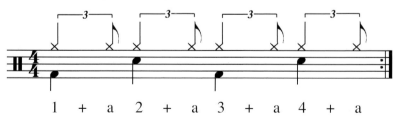

Now the snare is added here to beat 1 of groups 2 and 4. You now have the classic shuffle groove. It may feel awkward at first, but practice can only improve your ability to play this essential groove.

Right: A drummer focuses on a shuffle groove—a fundamental element of the blues.

Fills

Once you have mastered the previous groove examples, you will want to add some spice to them. Fills add dramatic flourishes that punctuate the grooves and they can be used effectively within a song's structure.

A song can really come alive when the drummer plays a fill that just jumps out and you think "how good was that"! Although the job of the drummer is ostensibly to keep time and provide a compelling backbeat to a song, there is also great scope for embellishing the song with individual musical ideas. This is where you get your chance to stamp your personal touch on a song.

Although a great fill, like so many things, is subjective, there are ways to make sure you execute the right fill at the right time. Solid practice of the rudiments is an essential part of this. For example: play a simple eighth note feel groove, then, on beat 4, add a single stroke roll. There you have it—a fill. Try the following exercises to develop a feel for how fills can work.

Figure 1

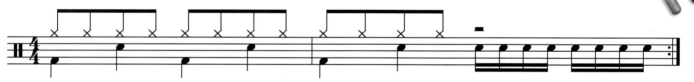

This first example consists of an eighth note feel groove with a single stroke roll sounding in sixteenths.

Figure 2

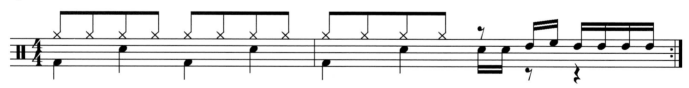

A similar example, but look out for the toms!

Figure 3

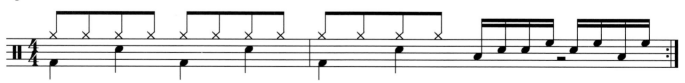

A snare fill.

Figure 4

Alternating toms and snare fill.

Figure 5

A groove broken up by two fills.

Figure 6

A variation of the above.

Figure 7

A two-bar fill. Here the fill lasts the entire length
of the two bars. Note the vertical bar line that
divides the stave. This separates bars one and two.

Figure 8

Second two-measure fill. Lots of alternating bass
drum, snare, and toms to negotiate.

Figure 9

Third two-measure fill.

Other Styles

The styles of drumming that can be applied to various genres of music are highly varied. The basic eighth and sixteenth beat grooves that you practiced earlier work well in rock-based music, but can also be applied to funk, disco, Latin, and many more. Here we will have a quick look at some of the different styles you might want to explore.

Jazz

In jazz drumming the ride cymbal is often used to mark out the time with the hi-hat. The snare and bass drum are used to add color to the music, which involves the player improvising to the accompaniment. The following is a basic jazz rhythm to try. If you are interested in this genre, then check out the work of noted players, such as Buddy Rich, Jack DeJohnette, Tony Williams, and Joe Morello, among many, many others.

Jazz Swing

Latin

Latin drumming and percussion is a huge and fascinating area to explore, which also poses its own particular brand of challenges to any player. There are many rhythms to learn: samba, bossa, songo, guaganco to name but a few. The examples below are in 2/4 time: "1, 2, 1, 2."

Bossa Nova

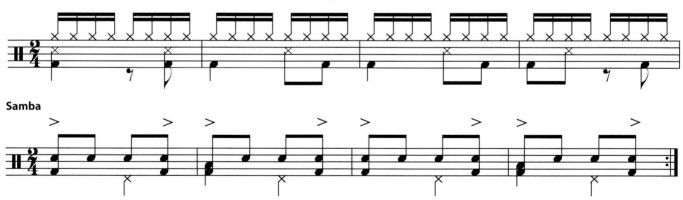

Samba

Note the accents on beat 1 and the second subdivision of beat 2.

Funk and Disco

Funk drumming is typified by the great playing of Clyde Stubblefield, Mike Clark, and Harvey Mason among others. Disco is an offshoot of funk that became popular in the late 1970s and was adapted in later dance music forms, such as House and Techno. Mainly played in 4/4, these grooves extend the basic eighth and sixteenth grooves with their syncopated placement of bass drum and snare.

Note the open hi-hat "kisses" (circled hi-hat notes). To play these, lift up your hi-hat pedal foot, then close it on the next beat.

Left: Harvey Mason is a past master of tight funk playing, which is brilliantly demonstrated on Herbie Hancock's 1973 album Headhunters.

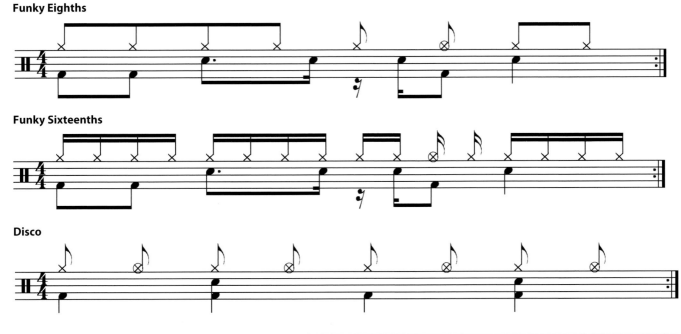

Funky Eighths

Funky Sixteenths

Disco

This is a deceptively simple groove that can be tricky to execute well. The emphasis is on accurate and metronomic accuracy. Often known as "four to the floor."

Right: Hi-hat syncopations are used extensively in funk playing. In disco, the hi-hat is open and closed every beat to create a distinctive pulse.

Final Pieces

If you've made it this far, then well done—you can call yourself a drummer! But remember, no matter how skilled you become, you will always be a student of the drums. You will never reach the point where you know everything—and that's the beauty of taking up a musical instrument. The journey of discovery never ends.

Here are two pieces that are more complex. They contain some of the concepts we have covered. Parts may frustrate you because they seem hard to master, but persevere. Try to "read" the pieces as you play, don't just memorize sections. It will be tough to begin with, but remember the mantra: "Take it slow!"

The second slightly longer piece begins with a fill and builds slowly. The first sections are sparse and are meant to create a mood—there is lots of space. As it progresses, it becomes more complex, but then at the end it becomes simpler again. It is designed to help your reading, so watch out for the odd dotted note!

Final Piece 1

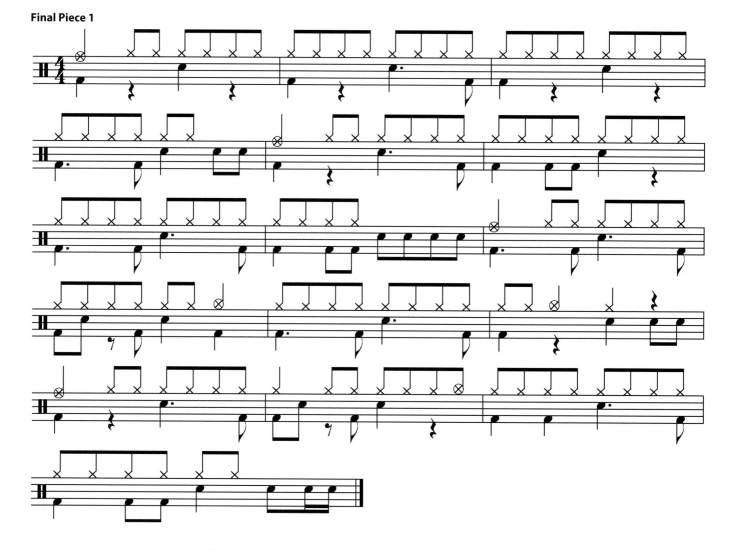

Final Piece 2

Epilogue

By now you will have discovered how rewarding playing the drums can be—and perhaps, at times, how frustrating! But, if you have taken your time and practiced slowly, you will have begun to master the basics. You will probably now want to take things further, whether as a hobbyist or as a potential pro.

Learning from a book is a useful place to start, but is only one element of the story. It is a good idea to seek tuition from a local drum teacher, who can assist your development with expert one-to-one advice. There is also a wealth of information available on the Internet—you can even participate in online tuition classes.

If you know any local musicians, or if your friends play instruments, there is great value in "jamming" with them. You may even want to form a band of some kind. Playing with others is an invaluable way to progress as a musician.

Listen to as much music as possible. Listen to professional drummers and try to work out what they are doing and, once confident enough, play along with them. It's a good way to learn and also identify which parts of your drumming technique need attention.

Above all—love music! What you put in determines what you will get out. As you become more competent, you will start to experiment and incorporate your own ideas. Music shouldn't be a technical exercise exclusively. Music has enormous power to inspire and move people and this includes drumming. Academic study is one way to acquire the language, but once you can talk in that language, think about what you want to say and strive to go beyond just conventional expressions.

I sincerely hope that this book has helped you to get started on your drum journey. Although it could not possibly cover every aspect of this huge

subject, I believe you now have the basic skills to allow you to take the next step forward.

Remember—it's up to you now!

Above: In a relatively short time you could be playing in a band—the ultimate aim for any budding musician.

Opposite: A student receives expert advice from a tutor. An experienced teacher can point the student in the right direction, providing very valuable encouragement and advice.

Right: Drumming is an exciting and rewarding pastime—it is also very good exercise. A drummer can burn off up to 600 calories an hour—the same as cycling or rowing at the gym!

Index

accents 26, 34, 42, 45
African drums 6, 10

backbeat 54, 63, 72
Baker, Ginger 11
balance point 33
bar lines 24
bass drum 11, 14, 15, 23, 55, 58, 62, 64, 66, 70
technique 57
beaming 23, 29, 30, 62
beat (groove) 52—67, 60—67
eighth note 53, 54—55, 56—57, 58—59, 61, 72, 74
eighth note alternate bass 56
eighth note alternate snare 58
sixteenth alternate bass 64—65
sixteenth alternate snare 66—67
sixteenth note 61, 62—63, 64—65, 66—67, 74
sixteenth hi—hat and bass 63
sixteenth hi-hat, bass, and snare 63
Bonham, John 12
bounce technique 41, 43
Bozzio, Terry 13
Bruford, Bill 11, 59
brushes 16

Carlock, Keith 13
Chandler, Dee Dee 10
Chinese drums 10
chops 37, 38—39
Clark, Mike 75
clef 25

Cobham, Billy 13
compound time 31
Copeland, Stewart 6, 13
counting sixteenths 62—63, 64—65, 66—67
crescendo 26, 50
cross-stick (X-stick) 23
cymbals 9, 10, 14, 15, 50, 67
crash 10, 14, 15, 23, 66
hi-hat 10, 14, 15, 23, 33, 54, 55, 58, 61, 62, 63, 64, 66, 70, 74
ride 10, 14, 15, 23, 74
splash 10, 15

decrescendo 26, 50
DeJohnette, Jack 74
diddle 44—45
Domino, Fats 30
double drag tap 48
drag paradiddle 49
drags 48—49
drumhead (skin) 10, 11, 15, 18—19
drumming techniques 21
drum 'n' bass 6, 14
drum set 6, 8—19
anatomy of 14—15
origins 10—11
drumsticks 6, 9, 16, 32—33, 39, 40—41, 43, 59
drum throne 15, 33
dynamic markings 26
dynamics 26—27

earplugs 17
electronic 14, 17, 19

fills 37, 66—67, 72—73
flams 46—47, 48
accent 47

floor tom 14, 15, 23
Foyeh, Toby 11
funk (and disco) 61, 62, 75

getting started 20—35
ghost notes 26, 34, 35, 46, 48
grip 6, 32—33
matched 32, 41, 43
traditional 32
Grohl, Dave 13

heavy metal 14, 57
heel-down method 57
heel-toe method 57
heel-up method 57

Japanese drums 11
jazz 6, 10, 11, 12, 14, 15, 16, 23, 51, 63, 74

Krupa, Gene 11

Latin 23, 74
Ludwig, William F. 10

Maddox, Fred 54
mallets 17
Mason, Harvey 75
Mastelloto, Pat 11
measure (bar) 24
metronome 17, 39, 40, 44, 47, 51, 55
military drummers 10, 38
Moon, Keith 11, 12
Moreira, Airto 13
Morello, Joe 74
multirods 16
musical stave 24—25

National Association of Rudimental Drummers (NARD) 38

Native American drums 10
New Orleans 10, 54
notation 6, 21, 22—23, 24—25
notes 22, 28—29, 42, 46, 48
dotted 64, 65
eighth 22, 28—29, 42, 46, 54—55
half 22
primary 48
quarter 22, 28—29, 46
sixteenth 22, 28—29, 42, 48, 64
thirty-second 42, 48
whole 22

paradiddle 44
-diddle 45
double 44
single 45
pedals 10, 57
bass drum 15, 33, 57
double bass drum 11
hi-hat 15, 33, 54, 62
Percussive Arts Society (PAS) 38
posture 32—33, 66
practice pad 17, 39

rests 23, 65
rhythm 6, 10, 22, 28—29, 30—31, 47
Rich, Buddy 12, 74
rimshot 59
Roach, Max 51
rock 6, 14, 17, 19, 54, 61, 74
rolls 37, 40—41, 42—43, 50—51
double stroke 42—43
five stroke 42

multiple bounce (buzz) 50—51
seven stroke 42
single stroke 40—41, 72
six stroke 42
triple stroke 51
rudiments 36—51
hybrid 38

shuffles 70—71
with hi-hat 71
with hi-hat and bass 71
with hi-hat, bass, and snare 71
single dragadiddle 49
single drag tap 48
snare drum 10, 12, 13, 14, 15, 23, 33, 51, 55, 58, 59, 62, 64, 66, 70
piccolo 14
Starr, Ringo 11, 12
strokes 6, 34—35, 44—45, 46, 48
down 35, 44, 45
full 34, 44, 45, 46
primary 48
tap 34, 44, 45, 46
up 35, 44, 45
Stubblefield, Clyde 12, 75
syncopation 66, 75

tension rods 14, 18—19
time signatures 24
tom-tom 10, 14, 15, 23, 66
triplets 30—31, 70—71
with hi-hat 70
with hi-hat and bass 70
with hi-hat, bass, and snare 70
tuition 7, 78
tuning 18—19

Williams, Tony 74

Author Acknowledgements

Simon Bridgestock would like to thank Nick Freeth for his valuable help and encouragement, and staff at Right Track Music School, Ashford, Kent, UK (www.righttrackmusicschool.co.uk), for their support and the use of music studio facilities. He would also like to thank Holly Bridgestock-Perriss, Emma Dodsworth, Daniel Jowett, and Oliver Scheuregger for demonstrating their drumming skills for the photography.

Useful Web Sites

National Association of Rudimental Drummers (NARD) *www.rudimentaldrumming.com*
Percussive Arts Society *www.pas.org*